NATIONAL GEOGRAPHIC

Tales from Timbuktu

PATHFINDER EDITION

By Marissa Moss and Janine Boylan

CONTENTS

Precious Pages. *This ancient book is a priceless treasure of Timbuktu.*

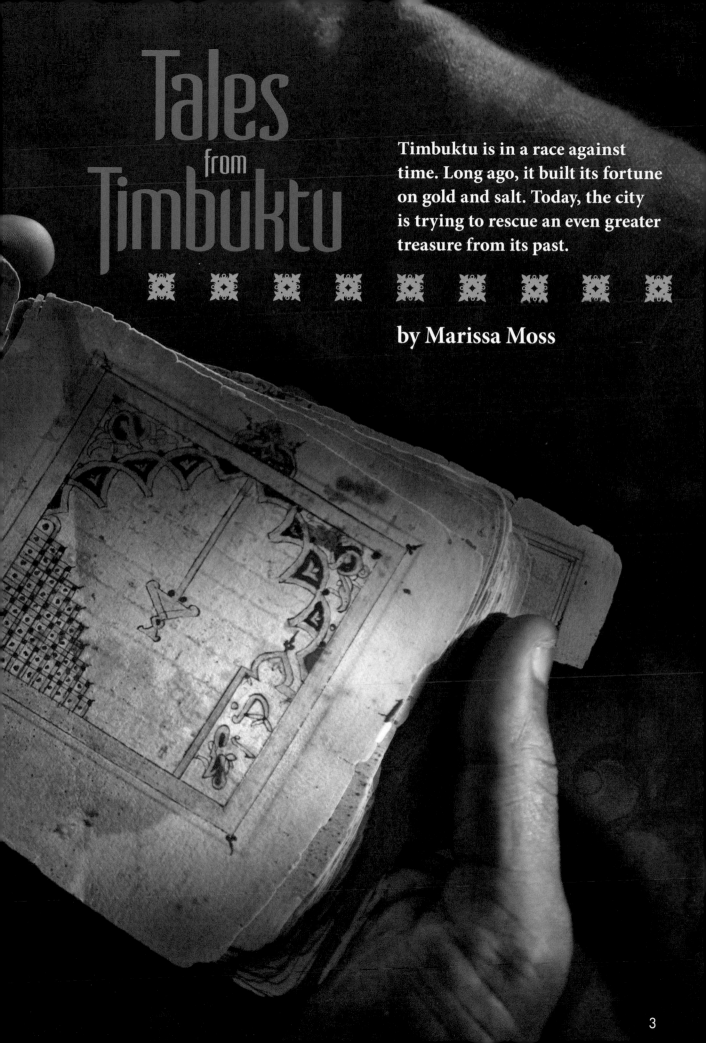

Tales from Timbuktu

Timbuktu is in a race against time. Long ago, it built its fortune on gold and salt. Today, the city is trying to rescue an even greater treasure from its past.

by Marissa Moss

Some say Timbuktu is the end of the world,

but it is not. It lies in the heart of the country of Mali, a place in Africa with a long history, rich with tales. The vast sands of the Sahara Desert spread to its north. The nourishing waters of the Niger River flow to the south.

Once upon a time, Timbuktu was Mali's most golden city. Step into Timbuktu's marketplace today and feel the hot sun. The sand under your feet is gritty. Look around at the low, clay-colored buildings. Some have spires jutting into the sun-bleached sky.

Women in brightly colored skirts walk by, and you pass baskets filled with white rice and millet. You see red tomatoes and tan peanuts, rubber sandals, and plastic buckets. A fire burns orange in a clay oven, where a woman bakes fresh bread.

Bread Baker. *A woman in Timbuktu bakes bread in a traditional oven.*

Center of Learning. *Centuries ago, thousands of students studied at the Sankore mosque in Timbuktu.*

4

Bringing the Past to Life

In one part of the market, a very old man prepares to tell a story. You sit in front of him as he squats and pours you a cup of tea. He is a *griot*, or a traditional storyteller.

If you lived in Mali, this is one way you would learn about your country. Griots chant about kings and magicians. They sing about wars and journeys that took place in the past. History has been shared this way in Mali for countless generations.

This griot has told the story of Timbuktu's famous past a thousand times. Listen as he takes you back 700 years, to the 14th century. He begins the way he always does…

"Long, long ago, when Mali was a powerful kingdom, there was a great king named Mansa Musa. He made Timbuktu into the City of Gold. Walk around Timbuktu today, and you can still see the enormous mosque that the king built. The gold from the past is gone; yet another **treasure** remains."

Golden King. *A map of Africa made in Spain in the 1300s shows Mansa Musa.*

GOLD AND SALT

Gold and salt helped make Timbuktu rich. Miners dug gold out of mines in the southern part of the Mali Empire, and workers collected salt in the northern desert. They dug 23-kilogram (50-pound) blocks of salt up from under the sand.

It's easy to understand why gold was so valuable, but why did people value salt? Here's the answer: People wanted salt because it made food taste better. They also used salt to **preserve** food, making it last a long time without rotting. Back then, salt was hard to find in other parts of the world. People in Mali even used salt as money. It once was worth as much as gold!

Traders carried gold, salt, and other goods from Mali to sell in other places. They brought back spices, silk, and more.

Timbuktu, where the desert met the river, was in the perfect place to become Mali's biggest trading center. It was the crossroads for traders traveling trade routes north to Europe and Egypt or south to the Atlantic Ocean.

Traders rowed up and down the Niger River and crossed the desert in caravans of camels. From all the goods they sold, the king collected taxes, or money, so the kingdom became very rich.

Traveling to Timbuktu. *This artwork shows explorers going to Timbuktu in the 1800s.*

Golden Journey

The griot continues the story. "Mansa Musa was a wise and religious man. He made a pilgrimage to Mecca, a holy city. He traveled with thousands of followers and a treasure-load of gold. He went with his first wife and 500 of her servants."

"A line of 100 camels stretched as far as the eye could see, with each camel carrying 140 kilograms (309 pounds) of gold. Five hundred servants, each holding a heavy staff of gold, followed the camels. Thousands of ordinary people walked behind them. It looked like an entire city winding through the desert."

A New Treasure

"The journey took Mansa Musa a year. Everywhere he went, the king gave away his gold. When he reached Mecca, the gold was gone, but that didn't matter to Mansa Musa. Now his name was golden. When people heard about Timbuktu, they didn't think of mud huts. They imagined a city shining like gold."

"Mansa Musa gave away his gold, but he brought back a different treasure: knowledge. The camels carried books about medicine, math, law, and more subjects. **Scholars** returned with the king. So did an architect, or building designer. They helped turn Timbuktu into a city of mosques, libraries, and schools. It had been a center of trade, but now it was also a center of learning, culture, and religion. Timbuktu truly was a golden city," the griot says.

Recovering the Past

It has been hundreds of years since Mansa Musa ruled. Mali fell on hard times. Trade routes moved from the desert to the ocean, and other countries wanted to rule Mali. Some started battles and caused great **damage**.

In 1960, Mali finally became an independent country. Although no other country controls it, today it is one of the world's poorest nations. Yet it still has a priceless treasure—books from its golden past.

Many of the ancient books are wrapped in leather. Some are written on paper; others on tree bark or gazelle skin. Many are handwritten in flowing Arabic letters. Their pages are filled with ideas about stars and math, history and religion, and more. The books let us understand Timbuktu's brilliant past. Some of the ideas from centuries ago, such as those about making peace, may help us today.

But these books are in danger. Over hundreds of years, families have tried to protect them. Yet sand, weather, and even termites have damaged the books. Some crumble in private libraries and kitchen cupboards, while others lie buried underground or are hidden in caves. Some books rest in the leather trunks of traveling nomads.

Scientists are working hard to save the books. They are carefully preserving them by using scanners and special cameras to store the books on computer, creating a digital library. Soon scholars everywhere will be able to log onto the Internet and learn from Timbuktu's great past.

Take-Away Treasure

Before you leave, the griot shares an old Mali saying with you: "To succeed you need three things—the brazier, time, and friends."

The brazier is a stove to heat water for tea. Time is what you need to brew the tea, and friends are what you need to drink it. If you have good friends and good tea, can good stories be far behind?

Today, the griot told you a famous story from Mali's golden past. Ancient books and modern computers also are helping Mali share its stories with the world. As you sip the last drops of tea, ask yourself: What stories will *I* bring home from Timbuktu?

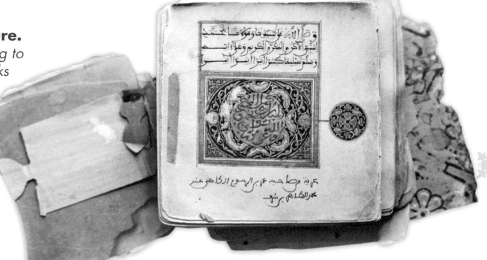

Priceless Treasure. *Scientists are racing to save precious books like this.*

Protecting the Past. *Researchers study a computer image of an ancient book.*

Growing Up Griot

BY JANINE BOYLAN

Nations are talking

Leaders are speaking

The day for which we waited has arrived

That is why we are saying:

*People of this united land,
    stand up, stand up with pride!*

— *Zolani Mkiva*

Modern griot Zolani Mkiva sang these words to celebrate an important South African leader, Nelson Mandela.

Griots like Mkiva carry history from generation to generation through songs. These artists collect and share stories in order to preserve them and to also link the present to the past.

Some people think the word *griot* comes from a French word. Others think it comes from an Arabic word. Still others think it must have African origins. While no one knows exactly where the word came from, it has been used for centuries to describe the praise singers from West Africa.

History Singers. *Griots from Mali wear traditional costumes.*

Family Heritage

In the past, not just anyone could be a griot. Griots are usually born into a griot family. Often griots marry other griots. That means a lot of griots have the same last name!

However, just because a child is born into a family of griots doesn't mean that he or she will become a griot. A griot is someone with a gift of song. Some children of griots become griots. Other children of griots chose other careers.

Griots are considered a special class of people. They have been trusted advisors for African kings and presidents. They have tutored princes. Griots help negotiate and settle disagreements. They also help teach people in the community.

Training

Griots train for years and years. As children, future griots learn to sing and play instruments. They might learn to play the lute, drums, or kora, a traditional 21 stringed instrument. They also learn their family stories and the history of their community.

Later, griots-in-training may study under older griots. This is when they perfect their art.

Some established griots like Kandia Kouyaté still spend as much time as possible with older griots to learn more. "You can't be a great singer or historian without listening to the old people," she explains. "I go to them to learn. I ask them things. I bring them kola nuts, as is the custom among us. I'm always with them, asking questions."

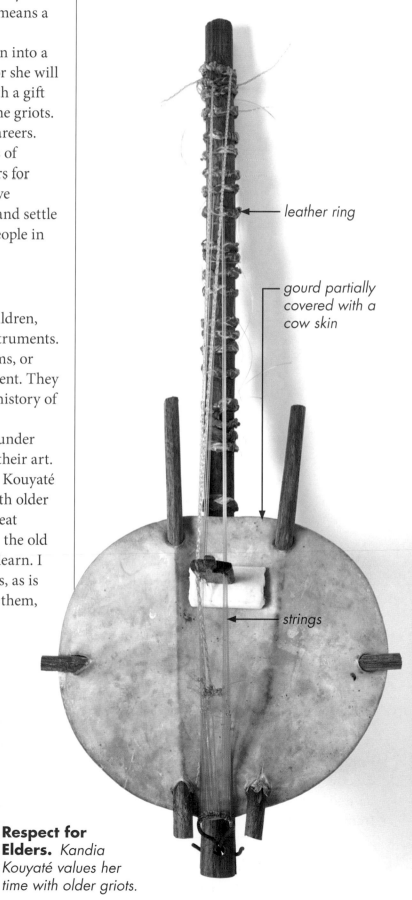

Kora Connection. *Griots often play the kora. People say it sounds a little like a harp.*

— *leather ring*

— *gourd partially covered with a cow skin*

← *strings*

Respect for Elders. *Kandia Kouyaté values her time with older griots.*

Rewards

Griots devote their life to their art. In addition to sharing and preserving stories, they also sing praise songs about their patron, the person who takes care of them. A patron may be the village chief or a wealthy business person. Griots get paid with gifts such as blankets, animals, houses, airplane tickets, cars, or money.

Sharing Stories. *Griots keep the past alive.*

WEB LINK

Visit **worldmusic.nationalgeographic.com** to hear Kandia Kouyaté and other griots.

Responsibility

Griots carry a lot of responsibility. Their songs are the records of births, deaths, and marriages in their community. They tell of battles and hunts, and they pass along folktales. Villagers depended on a griot to continue to record current events while also preserving their community's history.

Because a griot's songs preserve this essential information, the griot holds a very important position in the community. Griots recognize this and feel a great responsibility to always speak the truth.

Zolani Mkiva understands the responsibility. He says that he always has "to give careful consideration before participating in an event and frequently [will] research the topic at hand, [and] maybe prepare a specific framework for a recital."

New Song. *Zolani Mkiva is one of the youngest griots in South Africa.*

Performances in the Past

In the past, griots' songs were not recorded. Every performance was unique, with griots making up the words as they sang them. The stories might be told over and over again, but the actual words were allowed to change with each performance.

Griots Today

Griots like Kandia Kouyaté have decided to share their art with the world. They give concerts around the globe. They perform with other artists. They sing different types of songs.

They also record their music. You no longer have to go to West Africa to hear a griot. Their songs are just a click away.

Global Sound. *Kora player Toumani Diabate performs his songs around the world.*

Stories to Tell

Listen as the griots tell their tales. Then answer these questions.

1 Why was Timbuktu an important city in the 14th century?

2 What treasure did King Mansa Musa bring to Timbuktu? Describe how he did this.

3 What has damaged the books of Timbuktu? What are scientists doing to save them?

4 How do griots learn their art? How do griots change their art for people today?

5 Why is it important to protect books and stories?